Creating Effective Boards and Committees

Implement the BCem model to optimise director effectiveness

Endorsements

The position of a director is indeed very onerous. It requires many attributes and a multiplicity of talents and skills. It is insufficient simply to possess the required attributes, talents and skills; It is equally important for the director to have the ability to apply these attributes inpractise. The combination of all this is very daunting even for experienced directors; how more so for those whose entry into the corporate world as directors has only just begun. A great service has been done to these people by Sindi Zilwa in her latest book "Creating Effective Boards and Committees". In this book Sindi has compiled an admirable collection of tools which should serve as an invaluable guide to people who serve as directors. It is, as was the case with her earlier book – the ACE Model on Audit Committees – a coherent, well formulated, logical model which sets out the required tools in a practical and comprehensive manner.

In addition, it is entertaining and easy to read. We are truly indebted to Sindi for this valuable contribution.

Michael Katz | ENSafrica Chairman

This book is presented in an easily accessible format to all those who serve as directors. All directors carry fiduciary duties but being a non-executive director is especially challenging as the incumbents of this office do not have the benefit of day-to-day involvement and yet they are expected to oversee and add value to the organisation. The author strikes the perfect balance between comprehensively addressing and providing practical guidance on relevant aspects that directors should be aware of whilst not overloading the reader with detail. This is a book which I recommend should be referred to by all directors on a continual basis.

Ansie Ramalho | King 4 Project Lead and former IOD CEO

In a complex and challenging business environment we as board members often wish for access to material that can assist to keep us focussed on the task and responsibility at hand. Industry information is really readily available – Sindi goes a step further to remind board members of their responsibility and how to execute to the mandate given by stakeholders. Its is a handy tool to all board members to assist us in being more effective , reminding one of the importance of the role but also ensuring that we add value to management and in so doing add value to staff and shareholders. Thank you Sindi , another valuable contribution from your pen.

Louis von Zeuner | Director of Companies

As a leadership coach, working frequently with young leaders in transition, I read Sindi Zilwa's new book with delight. I wish that I had this book when I was first appointed a director, many years back! It would have helped me enormously. I encourage all newly-appointed directors to read this highly accessible and engaging book, and use the guidance for growth and development. This book will enable new directors to learn about what they need to know about the business of the company, its people, structures and so on, and so contribute at a high level, very quickly!

Eileen Thayser | Leadership Coach and Psychologist

Throughout Discovery's evolution, excellent governance has been instrumental to scaling the organisation from entrepreneurial start-up to multinational institution. At the heart of such governance, lies smart and experienced Board members who are able to rigorously debate strategic opportunities and risks facing the business; achieving both economic and social objectives, and balancing short-term priorities with long-term sustainability. As the macro environments within which businesses operate become increasingly complex, the demand on Board and Committee members for constructive insight and dynamic governance is elevated. For new directors, such responsibilities can appear both foreign and daunting. This is where Sindi's book proves itself as an invaluable resource for new directors. It curates her extensive business and Board experience in the form of practical guidance to optimise preparation time and meeting participation. The tools and knowledge shared in the book make it a must-read manual for those seeking empowerment to become active influencers of company strategy and success – the cornerstone of economic and country growth.

Adrian Gore | Chief Executive | Discovery

As the journey of South Africa's quest for inclusive economic growth reaches new heights and uncovers new possibilities and terrains, more and more entrepreneurs and intrapreneurs of all hues will ascend the corporate hierarchy to energise the veins of commerce, and indeed, to set our country on a course to global greatness. For this to happen, for this revitalisation of the boardroom to set in, the new and the young will find their path from the stalwarts who have been there before. I can think of no better thought-leader and pioneer than Ms Sindi Zilwa, a professional of consummate merit, to light the path.

The saying goes that "balance is not something you find, it is something you create". Through Creating Effective Boards and Committees, the author has created a fine balance between Theory and Practice, between knowledge and participation, which is the central tenet of this book.

Written by one who has come up the ranks through merit, grit and grace, this manifesto of governance provides valuable counsel with authority and in a comprehensive manner. I have no doubt that this engaging book will prove to be a preferred and obligatory resource among those for whom integrity and excellence rank supreme, regardless of whether they are an apprentice or a doyen.

Philisiwe Mthethwa | Chief Executive, National Empowerment Fund, Director of Companies

I found Sindi Zilwa's book very easy to read and her Board & Committee Effectiveness Model very useful for all directors including seasoned ones. The validation and contextualization concept in elevating effective participation in meetings is spot on, and the flight plan analogy that reminds directors their restricted aerospaces every now and again can only enhance overall effectiveness of directors in any boardroom.

Jabu Mabuza | Telkom Chairman

The Board and Committee Effectiveness Model is a very innovative way that Sindi has sort to share her experiences and views about being a company non-executive director, a NED. I share most of her views and my own experience as a NED confirms that this journey is both exciting and burdensome. But increasingly, due to regulatory over-load, it is increasingly becoming difficult to attract people to become NEDS. In many years to come, we will most probably look back at this period and wonder how so much resource was wasted on over-regulation and not on business development and wealth creation and growth. Make no mistake, we need appropriate regulation because there are many crooks in companies too.

Companies are finding that they have to be extremely careful when it comes to communication with all investors. And so the NEDs do expect that their executive directors, in particular the chief executive officer must be good communicators. Although I must admit that there are some very successful CEOs who are hopeless communicators. But these are few in number. The big advantage for the NEDs is that they are not the official spokespersons for the company. So don't expect to join a board of directors to be the "communicator".

There is a debate whether a NED has to be experienced in the specific company whose board they join. The purists argue that preference should be given to this category of people. They prefer people who know the detail of the workings of the company. They would mostly want to appoint former executives of the company as NEDs. Whilst I do not wholly share this approach, it has some merit but is risky in that the tendency to protect the "wrongs" that they may have committed in the past is ever-present. However, an appropriate mix of the former "insiders" and "outsiders" has proven to be an excellence combination. But whichever the case might be, NEDs will find studying Sindi's book most helpful.

I highly recommend that NEDs read this book. I enjoyed reading and learning more from it. Director induction and training will benefit tremendously from this offering. Siyabulela!!

TT Mboweni | Former Governor of the SA Reserve Bank and a Director of Companies | Johannesburg

Congratulations on a wonderful book which I hope many copies will end up in most directors' hands.

Mpho Mamashela | SAA Captain | Former Board Chairman: Air Traffic Navigation Services SOC Limited

Sindi Zilwa's "Board & Committee Effectiveness Model (BCem)" makes an immense contribution to enhancing the quality and effectiveness of good corporate governance by providing a compelling road map and flight plan to new and established directors alike. This is the book to read for any board member who wants to be equipped with and/or understand the tools required to be effective in discharging their fiduciary roles. It is a must read for new and, needless to say, all directors who want to stay abreast and continuously improve their value add to the companies on whose boards they serve.

It provides a compelling flight plan which is an indispensable prerequisite to success in any area of endeavour in general, and in director effectiveness in particular. What is very special about Sindi's contribution is that it is based on her impeccable theoretical grasp of the issues as a professional combined with her immense wealth of experience on the boards of some of South Africa's powerful companies. She guides board members through the two phases of the BCem model which cover both the knowledge and participation elements which are key to director effectiveness. I wish I had this book before my first board role.

Kuseni Dlamini | Chairman Massmart Holdings Ltd

Sindi Zilwa has produced, at once, a very concise workbook but one which also encapsulates almost everything a new director (or even a more experienced one for that matter) needs to think about on entering the very complex world of being a director.

The workbook presents a model which is easy to follow. It covers the two key aspects which will ensure that the director adds value to the board as well as himself. One side of the model is the knowledge that the director brings with him to the board meetings. This is critical to his acceptance of the appointment otherwise he will add little of value to the board.

The other side of the model is that of participation once appointed...Possibly this is the harder part for the director to appreciate. The workbook provides useful examples and scenarios of what awaits the director and what needs to be considered so that appropriate decisions can be made.

For many directors the appointment to the board may be viewed as the main achievement. By using this workbook the role will be enhanced significantly and the real achievement is the contribution that the director can make to the benefit of the company. This is the corollary of improved decision making at the board level.

Every company secretary should ensure that all the directors have easy access to this workbook. Every chairman will appreciate the benefit that this brings.

Professor John Ford | Gordon Institute of Business Science

Creating Effective Boards and Committees

Implement the BCem model to optimise director effectiveness

by

Sindi Zilwa

publishing

2016

First published in 2016

ISBN: 978-1-86922-621-3
ISBN: 978-1-86922-622-0 (ePDF)

Published by KR Publishing
P O Box 3954
Randburg
2125
Republic of South Africa

Tel: (011) 706-6009
Fax: (011) 706-1127
E-mail: orders@knowres.co.za
Website: www.kr.co.za

Printed and bound: Mega Digital (Pty) Ltd. Parow Industria, Cape Town
Typesetting, layout and design: Reez Sewpersadh
Cover design: Reez Sewpersadh
Editing and proofreading: Laura Budler
Project management: Cia Joubert, cia@knowres.co.za

Dedication to my father

I feel very privileged to be able to write and dedicate this book to my late father Obbie Nkonki. Even though he died when I was 7 years old, he left me with permanent footprints of unconditional fatherly love, belongingness, self belief, protection as his last born, and values and guiding principles that still sustain and guide me 42 years later.

This is the man who was dedicated to his family and shared all his life's challenges, successes, and would bring home all his food favorites to share with us, always. He was excellent in spoiling us responsibly and was very predictable due to his unbiased and principled approach which was clear to everyone. He used to bring us fruit everyday, and years later (after his death), when we got hold of his old leather bag it was still smelling all the exotic fruits he used to bring us, bringing back memories of his love.

I enjoyed the full privileges of being his last born in every respect, from unlimited access to his time, energy, resources through to his plate of unsalted food that I always found delicious, because it was his. I also could not wait for him to come back home and report to him any unpleasant experiences I had during the day with all the confidence that he would deal with whoever spoilt my day decisively, and he never let me down. Every time anything went wrong I only knew that it was because he was not around, and without fail all would be sorted out on his return from a hard day's job, until, one day, he never returned.

My father invested his lifetime in creating a legacy as a husband, a parent, a builder and a man of God. He was unfortunate to have been a qualified builder at the time when South Africa had no opportunities for people of his colour, but he still made the best of the little that came his way. He could only do hand to mouth building projects, but he still managed to support his family, provided warm hospitality to any visitors or strangers in need, educate his children and created a platform to transfer his skills through on the job training to all his sons and to the futureless kids who crossed his and my mother's path.

My elder siblings share with me how loving and supportive he was as appropriate to their age, how firm yet tender he was in his parenting, and on how he was a visionary in setting a foundation for the future careers of his children, and how intelligent and independent thinker he was at a time when parents were challenged to provide firm and decisive leadership to their families, qualities which I could not have even noticed by the age of 7. He was focused on emotional wealth which made all of us to feel complete and wealthy spiritually and in our self-image and esteem, despite the limited resources we had.

As a dedicated Jehovah's Witness, he loved Jehovah with all his heart, his soul and his strength. He fully applied Deuteronomy 6 verses 5 to 9 in his life which emphasised the need for him to inculcate the knowledge of Jehovah God to all his children, to speak Jehovah's words in sitting, in walking, in lying down, in waking up and to tie them as reminders on his hands, as headbands in his forehead, on his doorposts and on his gate.

My father did just that in a dignified way. He also fully emulated Joshua when he said in Joshua 24 verse 15, "……….But as for me and my household, we will serve Jehovah." No wonder his family of 13 kids with their households and their next generations are dedicated Jehovah's Witnesses and love Jehovah in more than one way, more than 4 decades later, a real legacy very few can claim.

I feel blessed to have been his child and fully experienced his love and protection which shaped my balanced personality for the first seven years of my life. His love still carries me through and I can still feel the warmth of his hugs like yesterday.

Contents

Acknowledgments

I sincerely thank Jehovah God for enabling me to qualify as a Chartered Accountant at a very young age, at a time when this was viewed as extraordinary, making it possible for me to tap into opportunities that I would not have otherwise accessed, one of them being the numerous board positions I held which have enabled me to write this book.

Being a director can be viewed as fancy or rather as a wonderful achievement, whereas that is when the real hard work begins. A number of hours in a day are sometimes not enough, the intellectual and strategic challenges these positions bring are hard, and the emotional strain that comes with influencing transformative thinking required at board level cannot be underestimated. My family had to put up with all these hours and the emotional and mental strain I have gone through over the years.

I can't thank enough my husband of 23 years Sva who has continuously supported and encouraged me to excel despite any challenges or barriers I had to overcome. Thank you Sweetie for being able to count on your love and support always.

I am grateful to my daughters Liza (17) and Lihle (8) who always created space for mama to do what it takes to succeed, with love and affection. With parental coaching they have excelled in their roles and responsibilities and academically they have chosen to soar like Eagles in their respective grades. This really freed my time to follow my professional ambitions as these lovely daughters we are blessed with understand the true principles of teamwork, responsibility and support.

My thanks to all the senior directors I have served on various boards with, as this book is also a collection of my observations when I saw them excelling in action. Your wisdom and your years of experience you have generously shared openly with us has been great lessons for me, which I am now using to assist others to be just like you irrespective of their age.

My sincere thanks to Reez Sewpersadh, Alice Manye and Vuyani Ndlovu for their tireless efforts to assist me to finally get this book done. It was always overtaken by other deadlines but they managed to always pull it back on the line.

I thank the following wise people (Prof Michael Katz, Prof John Ford, Ansie Ramalho, Kuseni Dlamini, Jabu Mabuza, Philisiwe Mthetwa, Louis von Zeuner, Eileen Thayser, Adrian Gore, Former Governor Tito Mboweni, Captain Mpho Mamashela) who spent time reading my book and provided the preview testimonials used in this book. Your time and your honest feedback has been most valuable to me and to the future readers of this book. Nangamso!

This also provides me with an opportunity to acknowledge with thanks the following important people who took a risk a provided preview testimonials for my first book, The ACE Model – Winning Formula for Audit Committees. They are Honourable Minister Gigaba, Former Auditor General Terence Nombembe, Former SAICA CEO Matsobane Matlwa, Prof Michael Katz, Professor Wiseman Lumkile Nkuhlu, John Buchanan, Thuto Masasa, Sindi Koyana, Simon Susman, Mr Temba Zakuza, Advocate Nonku Tshombe, Brian Mungofa, Dr Steven Firer, Mahendrin Moodley, Mitesh Patel, Althea Grant, Siphiwe Sithole, Emma Mashilwane, Morne Kermis, Ahmed Pandor, Nyarai Nyatanga, Sangeeta Kallen, Dr Judy Dlamini, Noluntu Bam, Sva Zilwa, Phillip Armstrong. These added so much value to my first book that it can never be too late to acknowledge their contribution of which I am grateful for.

About the Author

Sindi Zilwa is a Chartered Accountant (SA) and a Chartered Director (SA). She is the CEO and co-founder of Nkonki Inc, a Registered Firm of Auditors and Advisors established in 1993 and is a non-executive director of various listed companies. She is also an author of the book. *"The ACE Model – Winning Formula for Audit Committees"*. This book is used by the Institute of Directors to train audit committee members in South Africa and is available on Amazon.com.

MRS SINDI ZILWA CA(SA), CD(SA)

Her director responsibilities include Non-Executive Directorship of Discovery Limited, Aspen Limited, Metrofile Limited and Gijima (unlisted). She is a member of the Audit and Risk Committee of all these entities and chairs the Social and Ethics Committee for Discovery Limited and Aspen Limited and is a member of the Discovery Actuarial Committee.

Her past Directorships include ACSA Chairmanship, Woolworths Ltd, Rebosis Limited, The Transkei National Building Society, The South African Mint, The SARB Cell Captive Insurance Company, WIPHOLD Limited, Telkom Limited, Primedia Limited, Ethos Private Equity, Institute of Directors, Alexkor SOC Limited, ATNS SOC Limited.

- **Some of the Awards she has received include** South Africa's Businesswoman of the Year by the Executive Women's Club in 1998, the Finance Category Award of the Eastern Cape Achievers Award which she publicly handed over to her then 80 year old mother to publicly acknowledge her influence on her ability to succeed in 2005. In 2008 she received the Woman of Substance Award from African Women Chartered Accountants and in 2014 Sindi won the Overall Woman Professional of the Year Award from South African Professional Services Award's Inaugural Awards.

Sindi is happily married for 22 years to Sva Zilwa and they have two daughters Liza and Lihle aged 17 and 8 years and is a Jehovah's Witness.

Preface

Behind every economy, whether thriving or sinking, is the world of corporates whose main responsibility is to implement a business model that creates wealth for its shareholders, and positive social capital with its stakeholders. This world of corporates is made up of individual companies, companies with individuals who collectively form the board of directors of each company.

The board of directors of the company has the sole responsibility of directing the affairs of the company in such a way that the company derives all benefits possible and secures its long-term sustainability. These individuals, the directors, have the mammoth task of applying their minds and making decisions that are not only beneficial for the short term, but also favourable for the long term future of the company.

The question has always been and still remains: how are these directors prepared for the main task of competent and adroit decision making? The answers are inadequate as most directors are taught what their responsibilities are, what it means to be a director and so on, but given insufficient practical guidance on exactly how to go about the board papers to glean optimal insights that will enable value add to the decisions that have to be taken.

I am talking from experience.

I had acquired theory from my background qualification as a chartered accountant and all other related materials available on the market, but yet nothing prepared me for the state of mind necessary when I was examining my very first board pack (in my 20s), the types of questions to formulate and articulate in order to intelligently evaluate what was in front of me, and also the manner in which I needed to participate in that meeting.

Around the boardroom table was a mix of both experienced and inexperienced directors, very old and young directors, and very loud and very quiet directors.

I could not tell which group would be more effective. Initially all I could do was to learn from the experienced and the loud ones. After a while, however, I discerned common threads amongst the most effective directors.

Creating Effective Boards and Committees resulted from packaging all the good reasons, skills and factors that allow various directors to excel. More than 20 years later, this model, comprised of two phases (knowledge and participation) remains relevant as it contains the information that certainly would have guided and assisted me as a young and inexperienced director. I am confident that even for years to come, inexperienced directors will find this a useful tool for navigating and effectively discharging their fiduciary responsibilities.

"Sindi Zilwa is in a privileged position which has clearly aided her in writing her book on Board and Committee Effectiveness and suggesting a model in this regard.

The privilege stems from her knowledge base, being a chartered accountant, and having practical experience of being a director of companies. One of the company's boards on which she sat was under my chairmanship.

Consequently I have been able to read that which she has written knowing that she has experience of both sides of the corporate coin, namely the academic and the practical.

A new director will receive an induction, usually from the company secretary but needs help in becoming an effective director. Effective in this context connotes understanding the issue and making a decision in the best interests of the company with intellectual honesty, leaving aside one's present needs and past experiences.

In her model Sindi has set out how a lack of understanding of critical issues such as one's fiduciary duties can result in one becoming an ineffective director. At the same time she points to inappropriate participation in meetings which includes an inability to listen, understand and interrogate the information before one.

People have a natural human inclination not to state that they do not understand an issue because they do not want fellow directors to think they are stupid. There can be nothing more stupid than being party to a decision on an uninformed basis or not understanding the issue at all.

The models developed by Sindi actually help a new director in using appropriate knowledge and participating on an appropriate basis at meetings.

A new director reading this book will be assisted in making a positive contribution at board and committee meetings."

Mervyn E King SC

Chapter 1

Introduction

Congratulations on your appointment as a board member! Most likely you will be joining one of the board committees soon.

A board appointment is a powerful achievement. It creates a platform for you to influence and direct the activities of a company and uphold its interest, and in the process, the decisions being taken under your guidance and approval will impact a number of stakeholders positively and negatively. You therefore have power and authority in your hands that must be used very responsibly, and very diligently, as any mistake you make will affect the other stakeholders, including the company itself.

What are the most common root causes of the mistakes of decision-makers?

The following are some, though not a comprehensive list, of the root causes:-

Inappropriate knowledge caused by:-

- lack of understanding of the fiduciary role as a director
- lack of understanding of the business of the company
- lack of understanding of the industry in which the company operates
- lack of understanding of the latest trends and developments within the industry, and
- lack of adequate preparation for meetings.

Inappropriate participation in meetings caused by:

- inability to listen and interrogate matters at hand
- inability to validate issues or to contextualise for the company
- inability to keep alert to red flags
- inability to follow through on matters previously raised, and
- inability to provide guidance and resourcefulness when necessary.

It is important to plan to succeed at the beginning of each journey. As you are starting a journey towards being a director, you need to be prepared.

We all need a flight plan before taking off for greater heights in our lives, which is, in your case, as an effective director and board committee member.

Chapter 2

The Flight Plan

Prior to take-off, we all need a flight plan. Every step we take as professionals, we take in order to succeed in a big way; hence, I apply this analogy of a flight. No one becomes excited just to be able to walk the mundane path; rather, we give it all we have, we leap, we fly, to ensure that we excel and leave valuable footprints for those we reach through our respective roles.

Since every commercial airline flight begins with a flight plan, as a board member, you too must prepare for take-off, begining your journey as a director with a flight plan.

What does a simple flight plan achieve?

Here are a dozen benefits, but there are numerous others:-

✈   It forces you to acknowledge your current position;

✈   It enables you to determine your destination with clarity;

✈   It broadens your understanding of the type of aircraft you will be flying and its limitations;

✈   It allows you to evaluate the different routes that are available to you;

✈   It enables you to decide on the shortest possible route and allocate time to it;

✈   It forces you to calculate the minimum and maximum amount of jet fuel you will need to deal with the contingencies;

✈   It enables you to gauge the best altitude for flying given the type of aircraft, the weather and the fuel savings you wish to achieve;

✈   It guides you to avoid the restricted airspaces, the no-go zones;

✈   It enables you to determine the geographic aerospace you will utilise and the various frequencies needed to communicate effectively;

✈   It allows you to ascertain the different types of airports to use when emergencies arise;

✈   It prepares you to adjust your speed or direction in unpredictable wind;

✈   It helps you to establish your reaction to stormy weather, minimising turbulences.

Having mentioned a dozen reasons why a flight plan is necessary, I need to bring the analogy back into the boardroom as you are about to take-off.

Your Current Position	This enables you to realistically assess your level of readiness to be an effective board member.
Your Destination	This enables you to set a goal for yourself on the level of effectiveness you hope to achieve and on defining your success in this board.
The Type of Aircraft	The type of aircraft you fly represents yourself, your strengths and weaknesses. This aircraft needs to be evaluated in line with what is required.
Understanding the Different Routes	You need to understand the various ways by which you can increase your understanding of the company and related issues to enhance your effectiveness.
Selecting the Shortest Possible Route	As a board member, you need to decide on the best route necessary to quickly reach your destination, that of being an effective board member. The knowledge you need to obtain is of utmost importance when it comes to selecting a possible route.
Minimum and Maximum Jet Fuel Needed	The jet fuel represents your time. You need to carefully assess how much time you need to fulfil your responsibilities as a board and board committee member.

| **Best Altitude Level** | The altitude level represents the areas in which you must excel: business strategy, governance, finance, controls environment, etc. You need to know these areas upfront so that you can invest time in sharpening your knowledge to excel at your altitude level. |

| **Restricted Airspaces** | This represents the laws and regulations to which your company must comply, the do's and don'ts of being a non-executive director, and the general protocol you must observe. |

| **Geographic Aerospace** | This represents the areas in which you are permitted, that is, your territories. These might include the pre-meetings, and consultations with management and the chairman of the board. |

| **Airports for Emergencies** | There will be emergencies en route to becoming an effective director (what you thought would be easy to achieve might not). You need to be aware of alternative solutions that will increase the chances of meeting the overall objectives. There is no one route for all. |

| **Adjusting to the Winds** | This represents your approach in resolving areas of differences with management or other board members. There is no one way to resolve them. You must always be capable of reducing or accelerating your speed, taking into account the direction and velocity of the wind. |

| **Navigating Turbulences** | In all flights, there will be turbulences of sorts. You must learn to fasten your seatbelt when things are tough, because your ideas, if implemented successfully, would make a difference to those who cannot be heard. Abandoning your flight means you are abandoning the stakeholders who depend on your success for their survival (e.g. transformation issues). |

As you embark on this flight to a destination of effectiveness, please fasten your seatbelt and allow me to introduce you to the Board & Committee Effectiveness Model (BCem).

Chapter 3

The Board & Committee Effectiveness Model (B6em)

In this book, I equip you with the tools you require to know what is expected of you as a board member, and to be able to identify when you are off track, thereby returning to the right track as many times as necessary.

This will be accomplished by introducing you to the Board & Committee Effectiveness Model(B6em). B6em has proved to be very effective in minimising, even eradicating, root causes of the most common mistakes of decision-makers, primarily making uninformed decisions. I will be introducing you properly to the two phases of B6em -the Knowledge phase and the Participation phase.

The Board & Committee Effectiveness Model (B6em)

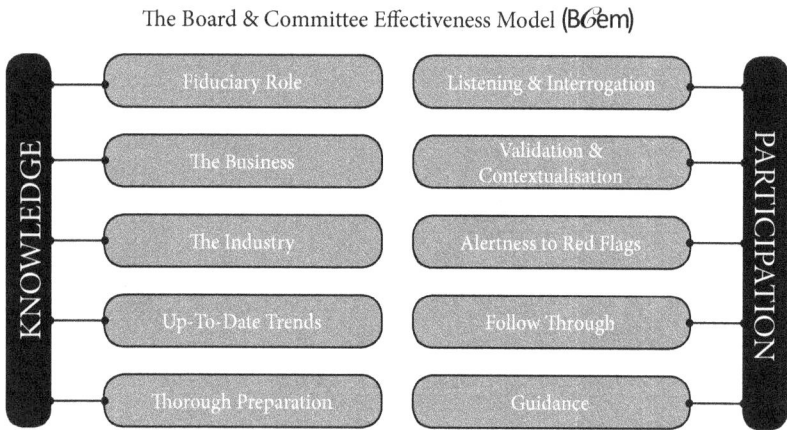

Part one of this book will be dedicated to Knowledge, with each chapter focusing on one element of the Knowledge phase.

Part two of this book will be dedicated to Participation, with each chapter focusing on one element of the Participation phase.

Chapter 4

Fiduciary Role

KNOWLEDGE		PARTICIPATION
Fiduciary Role	Listening & Interrogation	
The Business	Validation & Contextualisation	
The Industry	Alertness to Red Flags	
Up To Date Trends	Follow Through	
Thorough Preparation	Guidance & Resourcefulness	

As a director of a company, you need to have thorough knowledge of the fiduciary responsibilities.

1. What is this fiduciary responsibility?

According to the legal-dictionary.thefreedictionary.com, a fiduciary is defined as

"An individual in whom another has placed the utmost trust and confidence to manage and protect property or money. The relationship wherein one person has an obligation to act for another's benefit."

In this case, the company places the utmost trust and confidence in you as the director to manage and protect its interest. This is an enormous and serious responsibility.

The free dictionary continues to explain as follows:-

"A fiduciary relationship encompasses the idea of faith and confidence and is generally established only when the confidence given by one person is actually accepted by the other person. Mere respect for another individual's judgment or general trust in his or her character is ordinarily insufficient for the creation of a fiduciary relationship. The duties of a fiduciary include loyalty and reasonable care of the assets within custody. All of the fiduciary's actions are performed for the advantage of the beneficiary."

Now that you have accepted your role as a director, every action you will be taking within that company must be meant as an advantage to the company as the beneficiary. Again I emphasise: this is a huge responsibility which should not be taken lightly.

The common law duties of a director are a unique set of obligations which are owed by the directors to the company they serve, and are therefore mainly protective of the company.

In carrying out your duties as a director, you will be more than just effectively acting as an agent for the company, you are also fiduciaries vis-à-vis the company, which means that you also have a duty to protect the company's interests.

These duties are collectively called 'fiduciary duties'.

Set out below are the categories into which the common law duties of directors are generally divided.

A. Duty to Exercise Care, Skill and Diligence

As a director you must perform your duties and functions with care and skill, and you must carry out your duties diligently.
Diligence carries with it the necessity to devote a reasonable amount of time and attention to the company's affairs. Failure to exercise proper diligence may indicate that a director has acted negligently and, in some cases, may even indicate that a director has acted dishonestly.

For example, if as a director you had reason to suspect that an employee is defrauding the company, failure to investigate the matter might amount to connivance in the fraud and, consequently, to dishonesty.

B. Duty to Act in the Best Interests of the Company

This is generally regarded as the most important of all the fiduciary duties of directors. It dictates that as a director, you owe your duty to the company you serve, and no one else.

C. Duty to Act Within Their Powers and for a Proper Purpose

The powers granted to directors can only be used for the purposes for which they were granted; directors cannot, for example, exercise their powers for an unauthorised or improper purpose. This occurs essentially where directors act beyond their authority or beyond any limitation placed on their authority by the Act, the common law or the Memorandum of Incorporation. A director must always act honestly.

D. Duty to Exercise Independent Judgment

As a director, you must always exercise an independent, unbiased judgment in reaching the decisions you make for the company.

E. Duty to Avoid Conflicts of Interest

As a director, you must not place yourself in a position in which you have, or may have, a personal interest or a duty to another which conflicts, or may conflict, with the interests of the company or with your duties to the company. As a director, you cannot prefer your own interests above those of the company.

2. Standards of Director's Conduct

Section 76(3) of the Companies Act 71 of 2008 codifies what are generally regarded as the most important common law duties of directors.

It provides that, subject to sections 76(4) and (5), a director, when acting in that capacity, must exercise the powers and perform the functions of director:

a)   in good faith and for a proper purpose;
b)   in the best interests of the company; and
c)   with the degree of care, skill and diligence that may reasonably be expected of a person (i.e. an objective test)

    (i)   carrying out the same functions in relation to the company as those carried out by that director; and

    (ii)   having the general knowledge, skill and experience of that director.

These standards of conduct are, however, significantly ameliorated by sections 76(4) and (5).

3.   The Business Judgement Rule

Section 76(4)(a) contains what may well prove to be the most frequently invoked defence by a director when faced with an allegation that the director has breached his duties to the company.

It is a statutory version of the so-called 'business judgment test', which originated in the USA. It provides that, in respect of any particular matter arising in the exercise of the powers or the performance of the functions of director, a particular director will be deemed to have acted in the company's best interests and to have performed his functions with the necessary care, skill and diligence in respect of a particular matter (i.e. a director will be deemed to have discharged all the duties set out in section 76(3), other than the duty to act in good faith and for a proper purpose), if the director:

(i)   has taken reasonably diligent steps to become informed about the matter; and
   (aa) either had no material personal financial interest in the subject matter of the decision;
   (bb) or disclosed such personal financial interest to the board or shareholders in compliance with section 75; and
(ii)   made a decision, or supported the decision of a committee or the board, with regard to that matter; and
(iii) had a rational basis for believing, and did believe, that the decision was in the best interests of the company.

In short, if a director who has no financial conflict of interest in a matter takes reasonable steps to become informed of the matter but nevertheless, and in good faith, then makes an incorrect decision in relation to it, the director cannot be held liable for contravening sections 76(3)(b) or (c) if there was a rational basis for his decision.

The rationale for the business judgment test is that, since all businesses have to take some financial risk in order to grow and prosper, directors should be encouraged to take carefully considered, reasonable risks, and should not have to worry about being held personally liable for doing so.

4. Reliance on Others

Sections 76(4)(b) and 76(5) are largely a codification of the common law in relation to reliance by directors on the actions and information of others in discharging their duties.

Section 76(4)(b) provides that, in respect of any particular matter arising in the exercise of the powers or the performance of the functions of a director, a particular director of a company is entitled to rely on:

(i)   the performance by any of the persons referred to in section 76(5) or persons to whom the board may reasonably have delegated, formally or informally by course of conduct, the authority or duty to perform one or more of the board's functions that are delegable under applicable law; and

(ii)   any information, opinions, recommendations, reports or statements, including 'financial statements' and other financial data, prepared or presented by any of the persons specified in section 76(5).

Section 76(5) provides that, to the extent contemplated in section 76(4)(b), a director is entitled to rely on:

(a)   one or more employees of the company whom the director reasonably believes to be reliable and competent in the functions performed or the information, opinions, reports or statements provided; or

(b)   legal counsel, accountants or other professional persons retained by the company, the board or a committee as to matters involving skills or expertise that the director reasonably believes are matters within the particular person's professional or expert competence or as to which the particular person 'merits confidence'; or

(c) a committee of the board of which the director is not a member, unless the director has reason to believe that the actions of the committee do not 'merit confidence'.

Section 76(5) could be used as a barometer against which the standards of skill, care and diligence required of a director in terms of section 76(3)(c) are measured.

5. Other Fiduciary Duties

Section 76(2)(a) codifies two common law fiduciary prohibitions or 'negative duties'. It provides that a director of a company must not use the position of director, or any information obtained while acting in the capacity of a director to:

(i) gain an advantage for the director, or for another person other than the company or a wholly-owned subsidiary of the company; or

(ii) knowingly cause harm to the company or a subsidiary of the company.

The references to a 'subsidiary' expand the scope of these common law duties because a director owes no common law fiduciary duty to a subsidiary, whether wholly-owned or not.

Section 76(2)(b) reflects a director's common law fiduciary duty to disclose information which is material to the company. It provides that a director must communicate to the board at the earliest practicable opportunity any information that comes to the director's attention, unless the director:

(i)   reasonably believes that the information is immaterial to the company or that the information is generally available to the public, or known to the other directors; or

(ii) is bound not to disclose that information by a legal or ethical obligation of confidentiality.

The fiduciary duties of a director are further emphasised through section 75 of the Act which deals with a director's personal financial interest. The section requires a director to declare any personal financial interest which has to be considered for any decision where this interest is implicated.

Furthermore, these duties are included in section 77 of the Act which deals with a director's liability. The director becomes liable for breach of fiduciary duties as per section 76 for any loss or damage to the company. The director may be indemnified through the director's liability insurance subject to the conditions of the Act.

There are various judgments in case law which have found against directors.

The most important recent case quoted internationally is Australian Securities and Investments Commission v Healey.[1] This judgment emphasises the importance of directors in taking their functions seriously, not over relying on others (especially the audit committee), having basic financial knowledge, to scrutinising board submissions very carefully, and applying their mind when taking critical decisions.

1

"The Civil Lawyer." : The Centro Matter: ASIC v Healey [2011] FCA 717 and Breach of Director's Duties. N.p., n.d. [Online available] <http://www.the-civil-lawyer.net/2011/06/centro-matter-asic-v-healey-2011-fca.html>. [Accessed 4 May 2016].

Below is an extract from the case:

a. "The directors are intelligent, experienced and conscientious people. There has been no suggestion that each director did not honestly carry out his responsibilities as a director.

   However, I have found, in the specific circumstances of the subject of this proceeding, that the directors failed to take all reasonable steps required of them, and acted in the performance of their duties as directors without exercising the degree of care and diligence the law requires of them...

b. In the light of the significance of the matters that they knew, they could not have, nor should they have, certified the truth and fairness of the financial statements, and published the annual reports in the absence of the disclosure of those significant matters.

   If they had understood and applied their minds to the financial statements and recognised the importance of their task, each director would have questioned each of the matters not disclosed. Each director, in reviewing financial statements, needed to enquire further into the matters revealed by those statements.

c. The central question in the proceeding has been whether directors of substantial publicly listed entities are required to apply their own minds to, and carry out a careful review of, the proposed financial statements and the proposed directors' report, to determine that the information they contain is consistent with the director's knowledge of the company's affairs, and that they do not omit material matters known to them or material matters that should be known to them.

d. A director is an essential component of corporate governance. Each director is placed at the apex of the structure of direction and management of a company. The higher the office that is held by a person, the greater the responsibility that falls upon him or her.

The role of a director is significant as their actions may have a profound effect on the community, and not just shareholders, employees and creditors.

e. This proceeding involves taking responsibility for documents effectively signed-off by, approved, or adopted by the directors. What is required is that such documents, before they are adopted by the directors, be read, understood and focused upon by each director with the knowledge each director has or should have by virtue of his or her position as a director.

I do not consider this requirement overburdens a director, or as argued before me, would cause the boardrooms of Australia to empty overnight. Directors are generally well remunerated and hold positions of prestige, and the office of director will continue to attract competent, diligence and intelligent people.

f. The case law indicates that there is a core, irreducible requirement of directors to be involved in the management of the company and to take all reasonable steps to be in a position to guide and monitor. There is a responsibility to read, understand and focus upon the contents of those reports which the law imposes a responsibility upon each director to approve or adopt.

g. All directors must carefully read and understand financial statements before they form the opinions which are to be expressed in the declaration required by S295(4). Such a reading and understanding would require the director to consider whether the financial statements were consistent with his or her own knowledge of the company's financial position.

This accumulated knowledge arises from a number of responsibilities a director has in carrying out the role and function of a director. These include the following: a director should acquire at least a rudimentary understanding of the business of the corporation and become familiar with the fundamentals of the business in which the corporation is engaged; a director should keep informed about the activities of the corporation; whilst not required to have a detailed awareness of day-to-day activities, a director should monitor the corporate affairs and policies; a director should maintain familiarity with the financial status of the corporation by a regular review and understanding of financial statements; a director, whilst not an auditor, should still have a questioning mind.

h.   A board should be established which enjoys the varied wisdom, experience and expertise of persons drawn from different commercial backgrounds. Even so, a director, whatever his or her background, has a duty greater than that of simply representing a particular field of experience or expertise.

A director is not relieved of the duty to pay attention to the company's affairs which might reasonably be expected to attract inquiry, even outside the area of the director's expertise.

i.   Nothing I decide in this case should indicate that directors are required to have infinite knowledge or ability. directors are entitled to delegate to others the preparation of books and accounts and the carrying on of the day-to-day affairs of the company.

What each director is expected to do is to take a diligent and intelligent interest in the information available to him or her, to understand that information, and apply an enquiring mind to the responsibilities placed upon him or her.

Such a responsibility arises in this proceeding in adopting and approving the financial statements. Because of their nature and importance, the directors must understand and focus upon the content of financial statements, and if necessary, make further enquiries if matters revealed in these financial statements call for such enquiries.

j. No less is required by the objective duty of skill, competence and diligence in the understanding of the financial statements that are to be disclosed to the public as adopted and approved by the directors.

k. No one suggests that a director should not personally read and consider the financial statements before that director approves or adopts such financial statements. A reading of the financial statements by the directors is not merely undertaken for the purposes of correcting typographical or grammatical errors or even immaterial errors of arithmetic.

The reading of financial statements by a director is for a higher and more important purpose: to ensure, as far as possible and reasonable, that the information included therein is accurate.

The scrutiny by the directors of the financial statements involves understanding their content. The director should then bring the information known or available to him or her in the normal discharge of the director's responsibilities to the task of focusing upon the financial statements. These are the minimal steps a person in the position of any director would and should take before participating in the approval or adoption of the financial statements and their own directors' reports.

l.   The omissions in the financial statements, the subject of this proceeding, were matters that could have been seen as apparent without difficulty upon a focusing by each director, and upon a careful and diligent consideration of the financial statements. As I have said, the directors were intelligent and experienced men in the corporate world.

Despite the efforts of the legal representatives for the directors in contending otherwise, the basic concepts and financial literacy required by the directors to be in a position to properly question the apparent errors in the financial statements were not complicated."

The above judgment points to the fact that as a director, you should be exceedingly diligent in adhering to the primary purpose of helping the company, and you should always make certain that you do not do anything to reflect detrimentally or jeopardise the company in any way.

Thorough knowledge and application of your fiduciary approach to the board, as you are supposed to, will enable you to be effective in discharging your fiduciary responsibility as a director.

Overall, the company is pleased to be represented by you as one of its directors, but with this privilege comes responsibility.

The general accepted norm is that if the audit committee recommends to the directors the approval of financial statements, the board would approve the statements on the basis that the audit committee has thoroughly reviewed them. Even though the audit committee has that role, what this judgement highlights is that despite the high level of confidence you have of your audit committee, you still need to apply yourself "diligently and intelligently" when reviewing those financial statements included in your board pack.   You need to also reflect on what could be missing in disclosure in these financial statements, given your knowledge of the business and what has been taking place throughout the financial year. The responsibility to approve the financial statements together with all its disclosures lies with you in your capacity as the board, that is the power you have which you must use responsibly.

Chapter 5

The Business

Knowledge of the Business

As you are keenly looking forward to starting your journey with your board, you need to remember to meet your company first and understand the business in which your company operates. This will entail more than just high level information; it includes a complete understanding of all the elements that connect to the nucleus of the company and its business drivers.

Some pertinent areas of knowledge include the following:-

The Legal Structure of the Company

A company's legal structure determines its legislative territory, so it is important for anyone associated with the company to understand its legal structure. The company's legal standing also defines the underlying fiduciary responsibility that each director commits to fulfil.

The Products and Services of the Company

It is important for you to understand the exact nature of the products and/ or services that the company offers to its customers. The inherent risk factors (e.g. obsolescence, easy pilferage) that emanate from the manufacture or retail of such products will allow you to better understand the risks that the company has to manage, that you now have a responsibility to manage as a director.

The Top Risk Matrix of the Company

As a board member, you should be aware of the risk profile of the organisation, as well as how the board has defined the risk appetite and risk tolerance limits. The company's Top risks and the corresponding mitigation plans have to be well understood. You have to understand the executives responsible for the mitigation plans and controls and the tolerance levels to which the residual risks have been reduced.

The Nature and Complexity of the Company's Business Processes

Some business processes might be very simple whilst others are quite complex. As a new director, you need to understand the level of complexity of your company's business processes and the risk factors that might be inherent in such complex processes.

The Organisational Structure of the Company

An organisational structure will help you to understand the management structure of the company as well as the degree of autonomy each business unit has, if any.

It is important to evaluate the organisational structure against the nature and complexity of the operations of the business to establish the alignment and the appropriateness of the financial reporting controls.

The Critical Skills Requirement of the Business

For any business to succeed it needs to be backed up by more than adequate skills required for this success. The current skills mix has to be aligned to the business needs in terms of the qualifications, depth of experience and the attributes required to make a difference to the company's strategic objectives. As a new director, you need to understand the availability of such skills internally and in the open market.

The Markets in which the Company Operates

This information is critical to understand both demographically and geographically to ensure that there is full awareness of the company's vulnerability to the various markets. As a director, you then need to keep alert to these markets.

The Legislative and Regulatory Environment under which the Company Operates

The legislative and regulatory environment is impacted by a number of different elements, some of which include:-

- the legal structure of the company;
- the nature of the industry in which the company operates;
- the nature of its products or services;
- the markets under which it operates;
- the competitive environment under which the company operates that attracts the competition laws;
- the regulatory bodies relevant to the company; and
- the licence to operate conditions.

In some industries these would include specific environmental laws with which the company has to comply. Full knowledge of the Regulatory and Legislative environment is imperative for you as a director.

The Compliance Function of the Company

Given the significant impact of the Legislative and Regulatory environment, it is important for a director to understand the capacity of the compliance function and its ability to provide assurance on critical areas of required compliance. As a new director, you must be informed if the company has had any previous transgressions that attracted fines and penalties, as this will enhance your ability to assess the risk.

The Key Business Drivers of the Company

Understanding the key business drivers of the company is critical since changes in these can either make or break the company's performance. Some possible risks that emanate from the movements in these business drivers can be mitigated whilst others cannot. Full understanding of that will be of great help. As a director, you should relate knowledge of the business drivers to the maturity of the organisation's governance structure and the risk profile.

Extent of IT Dependency

The extent to which the company is dependent on IT needs to be known and the complexity of the IT architecture needs to be simplified. This should be related to issues such as IT governance and IT risks based on the backdrop of issues like cyber risks, as these are currently posing serious challenges locally and internationally.

The Calibre of Management and Human Capital

It can be safely said that the success or failure of any business is a fair reflection of the calibre of management behind the wheel, including the quality of Human Capital.

Some of the key factors that can be considered include the following:-

- experience and competence in relation to the strategic goals of the company;
- successful track record;
- visible levels of integrity;
- teamwork;
- tone at the top;
- respect for governance; and
- ethical culture based on the organisation's value system.

The above influences how decisions are made within an organisation.

The Company's Governance Structure

This needs to be evaluated to establish how the company governance structures reflects the company's ability to embrace the spirit of corporate governance.

This can be done by evaluating the completeness of the structure in terms of the applicable codes of governance and legislation.

The concerns that keep the executive management awake at night should also be on your radar screen. As a director, you should be mindful of how these concerns are communicated and dealt with.

The Key Competitors of the Business

The company's vulnerability to competition (including lack of customer loyalty), and the knowledge of what competitors do better are excellent points to be acquainted with. In effect, the company's market share can provide a beautiful snapshot that can 'tell it all' so to speak.

The Company's Business or Corporate Plan

A business plan or a corporate plan that will provide the company's medium to long term goals should be assessed from the very beginning of your journey as a director. You should have access to the organisation's strategic and business plans and understand the business environment and SWOT analysis, the funding structure
and the company's ambitions over the medium to long term.

Business Model of the Company

The final framework issued by the International Integrated Reporting Council specifies the need for companies to communicate their business model as it illustrates their value creation processes. This involves communicating how the various forms of capital are utilised to create value for the organisation. It is important for any new director to understand the company's business model in great detail.

Chapter 6

The Industry

A director cannot be effective in a fiduciary role if the industry in which the company operates is not understood. Relating this back to the flight plan, not understanding the industry would be like flying without understanding the aerospace in which you are flying or the surrounding weather environment, which would be absolutely disastrous.

Directors are therefore encouraged to learn more about the relevant industry, as this will enable them to understand and contextualise all issues that are critical in facilitating sharp and informed decisions.

What is even more complex in today's world is that the industry boundaries are getting blurred and the competition is not clearly defined anymore. For example in the olden days there was never a competition with the post office, but today electronic communication is taking over. As a director therefore, you should not narrowly focus on the industry boundaries, but keep alert to new developments that would pose a threat to the continued existence of the company.

There are many ways in which a director can enhance industry knowledge, and there are various things to know about any industry. As a starting point, knowledge of the following is recommended:-

The Landscape of the Industry

Knowledge of the landscape of the industry in which your company operates will determine the following important factors:-

- the size of the industry;
- the major stakeholders;
- the competitors;
- its vulnerability to unions and the political climate;
- its elasticity to market and political conditions;
- the market share landscape;
- latest technological, legislative, health, environmental, and any other developments that might pose a threat to your industry;

- the company's ability to influence the market; and
- the view of the regulators against or in favour of the industry.

Knowledge of the above factors will enable a new director to relevantly apply intelligent and informed thoughts pertaining to issues tabled for the board.

The Maturity of the Industry

According to investopedia.com, a mature industry is defined as an industry which has passed both the emerging and the growth phases. It is important for a director to understand the maturity level of the company's industry.

When an industry has matured, certain key factors are present. Understanding these leads to greater appreciation of matters addressed at company level:-

- the availability of critical skills to support the industry;
- the level of barriers to entry are well understood if any;
- the regulator's approach to the industry is well understood;
- the mitigation controls for inherent risk factors are common cause; and
- the realistic levels of residual risk with which the industry is dealing are known and within tolerance levels.

The Track Record of the Industry

The industry's track record in terms of its success or failure rate is an indicator for insights into the critical risks and opportunities requiring continuous evaluation. How various competitors are hard hit by various economic fluctuations and legislation (e.g. competition's rulings,) are red flags empowering a director to stay alert in dealing with the company's business issues.

The Media Scrutiny the Industry Receives

Keeping up to date with this knowledge would enable a director to understand the existing bias, either for or against the industry. The reality is that the media is powerful for exerting pressure for change in any direction it wishes. Understanding this angle timeously would enhance the director's, and therefore the company's pro-activeness in dealing with the relevant issues that appear as cause for concern.

The Stakeholder Sensitivity

It is a fact that some industries have more stakeholder participation than others, and a director needs to be well aware of the following:-

- the nature of the stakeholders with which the industry is dealing;
- the level of stakeholder activism occuring within the industry; and
- the level of influence stakeholders have on the business of the company;

Clear understanding of this prepares the director for addressing the stakeholder engagement issues. It also enables appropriate monitoring of the relevant stakeholder framework adopted by the company.

The Industry Trends

Monitoring overall industry trends can be a powerful activity for any director, whether experienced or in-experienced. Numerous critical factors can be revealed through close analysis of industry trends:-

- innovations that threaten the survival of the industry;
- general decline or increase in the demand for product or service;
- reduced margins imposed at regulatory level;
- consolidation trends to take advantage of the economies of scale;
- additional licence to operate conditions;
- increased pace of technology applied by the industry to defend market positioning;
- awareness of how competitors thrive or fail; and
- increased obligations imposed on the industry (e.g. environmental obligations).

Knowledge of these trends is an essential ingredient in ensuring appropriateness of information for all directors and boards as a collective whole.

General Industry Threats

The industry might be exposed to various threats including the following:-

- national strikes;
- foreign products entering the market at less expensive prices;
- counterfeit products;
- new technology that threatens the obsolescence of the products;
- commodity prices or availability thereof;
- currency fluctuation issues;
- xenophobia; and
- global warming.

A director needs to be alert to threats affecting the industry in general as these are indicative of the threats that can mar a company's otherwise successful track record.

The Impact of Key Economic Indicators

Directors need to be mindful of the impact of changes in the key economic indicators such as the following:-

- interest rates;
- fuel price;
- unemployment;
- inflation, commodity prices, CPI, and PPI; and
- economic growth or recession.

Once these economic indicators are understood, the director's ability to evaluate the assumptions used by management for the company's budgets, strategic plans, growth and forecast is accelerated.

Significant Environmental Issues

Comprehending the complexity and the cost of compliance or non-compliance to the set environmental laws and regulations at an industry level is imperative for any director.

Industry Information

A director needs to make time to grasp the issues covered by the regulator in every annual report relating to a particular sector or industry. These reports normally investigate industry trends, the various areas of non-compliance that the industry has experienced, and the financial and non-financial achievements of a particular sector or industry.

Key generic performance indicators frequently included in these reports are valuable in assisting a company to benchmark its performances and achievements against the industry as a whole.

Whilst the individual company performance might be commendable on its own, knowing whether it is ahead of industry or lagging behind is an important factor to recognise, empowering any director to be a more effective board member.

Chapter 7

Up To Date Trends

This chapter is primarily an extract from my book,

"The ACE Model – Winning Formula for Audit Committees".

The world we are in changes every day, from the technology we rely on, to the regulations and the standards by which we are reporting or we are auditing. Keeping still in a flowing river would quickly make us irrelevant and obsolete. It is therefore critical that directors remain alert to all that is developing around them.

In addition to the critical developments that are taking place around the business which boards must attend to, there is a further need to keep an eye on emerging trends. These trends will assist in identifying emerging risks.

Based on the above analysis, this chapter, Up-To-Date Trends, will therefore cover the following:-

1.   the basic circle of knowledge for any director;

2.   keeping updated within the basic circle of knowledge and beyond;

3.   keeping alert to trends; and

4.   current news.

The Basic Circle of Knowledge

The basic circle of knowledge for a director will cover two areas:

- the core areas of knowledge (specialist knowledge and corporate governance)
- areas of literacy (areas requiring a solid working knowledge).

This is because as a director you cannot afford to contribute in some areas as an expert, and also on governance, and then be ignorant as to what is happening in other areas, thus placing 100% reliance on other board members for these other areas.

Therefore, irrespective of your core areas of knowledge, your basic circle of knowledge can be illustrated as follows:-

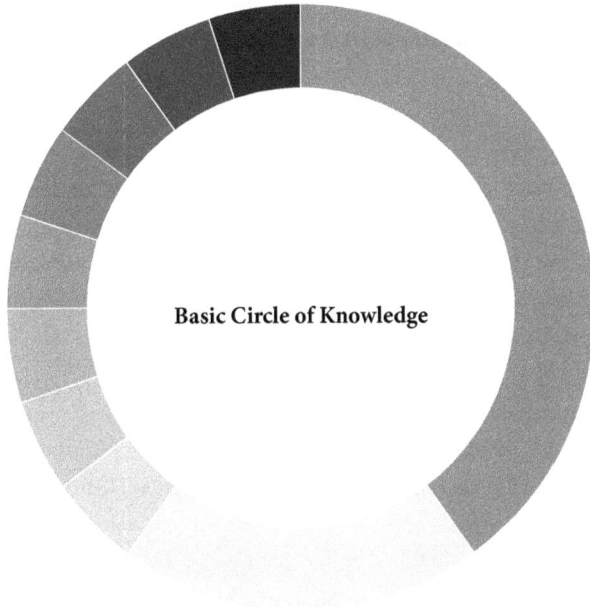

Basic Circle of Knowledge

Specialist Knowledge	Governance	Financial Literacy	Technical Literacy	Auditing Literacy	Compliance Literacy	Information Technology Literacy	Business Continuity Literacy	Tax Literacy	Risk Management Literacy

Areas of Core Knowledge

The specialist knowledge refers to the director's area of discipline, whether that be as an actuary, banker, chartered accountant, commercial lawyer, engineer, technology specialist, internal auditor, medical doctor or pharmacist, etc.

Knowledge of governance is a basic ingredient for anyone who qualifies as a board member. This involves general understanding of governance, the governance codes, rules that are applicable and best practice standards based on the exposure one has in the governance space.

Areas of Literacy

"I must judge for myself, but how can I judge, how can any man judge,
unless his mind has been opened and enlarged by reading."
- John Adams

Financial Literacy: This does not mean having expert knowledge of financial issues, but rather a working knowledge of the financial issues sufficient enough to understand the discussions and a willingness to enquire when in doubt. This can be summed up as being in a state of 'conscious incompetency' which enables you to seek answers when you need them, and to tell if things are not right.

If it does not make sense in the simplistic form, chances are it does not. The importance of basic financial literacy is supported by the judgment in Australian Securities and Investments Commission v Healey [2011] quoted in Chapter 4.

Technical Literacy: This needs to be sought at all times and as with financial literacy, this does not mean that you must have technical expertise, but rather a working knowledge of the technical issues affecting the business you are in. These technical skills vary from business to business and from industry to industry.

In an insurance company, for example, technical literacy means having working knowledge of the actuarial skills without pretending to be an actuary; in an IT based company, a working knowledge of the IT skills and services offered is necessary. Again, if the technical presentations don't make sense in the most simplistic form, chances are they don't make sense.

Auditing Literacy: This can be summed up as the ability to understand what your assurance providers (including both internal and external auditors, IT Auditors, environmental auditors, integrated assurance auditors) are telling you. As a director, you need to understand the implications brought about by the assurance providers' findings and the decisions that should be taken by the board as a whole.

A director must be satisfied that the necessary governance has taken place on the independence and objectivity of the assurance providers, as well as the integrity and completeness of the information being presented.

Compliance Literacy: Recently, compliance has become very important component of a director's array of responsibilities, with more organisations increasing capacity in the compliance function. This is mainly due to the increase in regulations and the resultant increase in monitoring by regulators. Compliance literacy can be summed up as the ability to understand the significance of the impact of the various legislation and regulations under which the company operates, the ease or complexity of the compliance process and the required monitoring thereof. All directors need to have a working knowledge of the compliance framework and how the risk of non-compliance is managed and mitigated across all levels of the organisation.

Information Technology Literacy: This refers to working knowledge of the IT systems and processes if the business is heavily dependent upon this literacy. A director needs to ask questions if something does not make sense in simple form, because chances are that indeed it does not make sense. IT governance is part of the information technology literacy and all directors should be comfortable with the level of IT governance maturity in their respective organisations.

Business Continuity Literacy: This cannot be ignored as business continuity reflects the greatest threat that faces any business. Despite your risk management strategy, if the black swan lands and the inevitable does happen, will that signify the end of the business or will this company be able to continue operating under different and temporal circumstances? This is a question every director should be capable of answering. Therefore, a working knowledge of what business continuity entails and the company's level of compliance with the available standards of business continuity will be beneficial for a director.

Tax Literacy: This is important because the impact of non-compliance with tax legislation, whether intentional or unintentional, is likely to be significant. Working knowledge of the tax requirements and the monitoring of compliance and status of tax returns submitted across the group is essential, requiring some degree of tax literacy for enhanced effectiveness.

Risk Management Literacy: This is critical to the effectiveness of the board in managing those issues which could hamper the organisation from achieving its objectives. For this reason, risk is the other side of strategy and cripples the sustainability of the organisation. If the director is illiterate concerning risk issues, the oversight capability to assess the relevance and thoroughness of the strategy, will be hindered.

In emphasising the need for various areas of literacy, the following extract from the judgement on Australian Securities and Investment Commission v Healey [2011] FCA 717 is relevant:

"A director is not relieved of the duty to pay attention to the company's affairs which might reasonably be expected to attract inquiry, even outside of the director's area of expertise."

Keeping updated within the Basic Circle of Knowledge and beyond

"Live as if you were to die tomorrow. Learn as if you were to live forever."
– Mahatma Gandhi

All the elements of the basic circle of knowledge are evolving and updating almost annually, in both the core areas of knowledge and areas of literacy.

"Never become so much of an expert that you stop gaining expertise.
View life as a continuous learning experience."
– Denis Waitley

As a director, therefore, you have to make it your business to keep up to date and sharpen your skills in the areas impacting your basic circle of knowledge.

There are various ways which you can, as a director be continuously informed:-

- attendance of annual update seminars relevant to your core areas of knowledge;
- subscription to relevant journals that will keep you updated;
- continuous online research using the skill required as a search word;
- participation in available educational and or training courses;
- attendance of relevant conferences and seminars;
- participation in technical committees, working parties and task forces;
- teaching and mentoring other board members as a way of continuous learning; and
- membership in relevant professional bodies.

K4- Keeping Alert to Trends

"I never predict. I just look out the window and see what is
visible – but not yet seen."
– Peter Drucker

A director must be alert to what is transpiring amidst the companies they serve to enable them to fully comprehend the issues at hand. The trends that must be monitored include both outward trends and inward trends.

External Environmental Trends

These are the trends that are emerging outside of the business which will definitely (or likely) have an impact on the business.

A director needs to notice and reflect on some of these trends.
Examples of such trends and reflective questions include the following:-

What **global trends** are taking place that might impact this business, e.g. global economic indicators, globalisation trends, or predicted recession in trading partners?

What **economic trends** are emerging which might positively or negatively impact this business (e.g. exchange rates, fuel prices, interest rates, or rate of unemployment)?

What **regulatory trends** are developing that could threaten the future of the business (e.g. claw backs by regulators, relaxation of barriers to entry, licensing of international players in other industries)?

What are the latest **fraud trends** emerging to which this business might be vulnerable (e.g. hacking of bank accounts or emerging syndicates)?

What **technological trends** are developing that might make the business lose its market share or become irrelevant (e.g. threat of laptops to desktops, threat of iPads to laptops, threat of cell phones to fixed line, or threat of wireless to 3G cards)?

What **litigation trends** are emerging which could be threatening to the business (e.g.
class action lawsuits, fines imposed by competition authorities, relevant judgments imposed by courts of law, environmental claims)?

What **labour unrest trends** are taking place and to what extent is the business itself vulnerable or immune to such strikes and possible excessive wage demands?

What **stock market trends** are taking place and is the company vulnerable to any of them (e.g. a decline in its share price if listed, impairment of listed subsidiaries, breach of debt covenants if losing market cap)?

What **competitor trends** are emerging that might pose a risk to this business (e.g. undercutting, buying market share, consolidation through mergers and acquisitions, strategic partnerships, international expansion)?

What **reporting trends** are emerging from other companies within the industry in which we operate, or from a group similar companies (e.g. listed companies)? Are we able to meet the set standards, and if not, what will it take for the business to emulate the best?

What **credit rating trends** are emerging both at sovereign and corporate level and what impact would those have on the funding costs of the company?

What **financial performance trends** are emerging from other companies which operate in the same industry and are we losing sleep to close the emerging gaps in terms of growth, margins, balance sheet strength and cash flow generation?

(Please note that the above is not an exhaustive list of external environmental trends.)

Internal Environmental Trends

Examples of inward trends are those that are emerging within the business itself.

As a director, you need to understand all inward trends, including the following:-

- **Declining margins** – these might indicate the company's inefficiencies so the root causes need to be analysed and investigated.

- **Previous transgressions** – these might indicate the company's lack of capacity to monitor compliance with specific laws and regulations.

- **Negative variances against budgets** – these might indicate management's inability to set realistic budgets, or their optimistic approach without a commensurate aggressive approach to meet them.

- **Company's track record in meeting financial covenants** – these might indicate the funding and operational constraints under which the company operates and the pressure to which management might be subjected in running the company.

- **Positive variances against budgets** – these might indicate an extra conservative approach that management is taking and possibly an attempt to entrench a performance bonus culture of exceeding targets that were unreasonably low in the first place.

- **Staff turnover** – a high staff turnover might indicate a deficient company culture and unacceptable management styles that rob the company of its institutional memory.

- **Types of audit findings** – these might indicate the culture of non-compliance to the internal control environment and a negative tone at the top which is not conducive to appropriate governance processes.

- **Revolving door for assurance service providers**– this might indicate that the environment is either high risk for auditors, a factor that must keep a director awake, or management that aggressively changes assurance providers the moment a difference of opinion arises.

- **Revolving door for senior staff members** – this might indicate critical issues that create pressure for these staff members, especially for those with a clean conscience who may find it unbearable to stick around.

- **Product returns or recalls** – this might indicate lack of quality control processes, staff sabotage, or future loss of loyal customers, the root causes of which must be investigated and acted upon.

- **Increasing costs to income ratio** – this might indicate an unsustainable trend and lack of management responsiveness to declining revenues.

- **Loss of market share** – this might indicate a lack of resilience in the management of the company and potentially threaten long term sustainability if the trends continue.

- **Back orders** – this might indicate lack of capacity for the company to cope with the demands, possible lack of security of supply of raw materials and loss of available revenue for the company.

- **Aging experienced workforce**– this might reflect a succession planning risk that the company might have, so a focus on ensuring that the depth of skills when lost will be replaced is critical.

- **Fraud hotline reports** – this might indicate the possible fraud trends, willingness of staff to report fraud and possible loopholes that need to be closed in the system.

- **Forensic reports** – this might indicate the susceptibility of the company to fraud, a weak internal control environment, a lack of screening ability for new employees, and a lack of fear to commit fraud due to a slim chance of detection.

- **Continuous restatement of results** – depending on the nature, this might indicate a need for the improvement of financial reporting integrity, inappropriateness of accounting policies, estimates and judgmental issues made. Underlying reasons should be thoroughly investigated with external auditor's assurance through specific reviews that can prevent further restatements in future.

- **Declining ratios** - the root causes of the declining ratios must be investigated and management action plans should be analysed for effectiveness.

- **Continuous attack by unexpected predictable events** – this might reflect the weakness of the company's risk management processes and the general inability of management to anticipate and mitigate risks.

- **Continuous refinancing** – this might indicate the short term approach applied by management, the financial difficulties the business is experiencing, or a weak management ability to deliver on promised turnaround plans.

Please note that the above is not an exhaustive list of internal environmental trends.

Current News

Finally, a director needs to take note of what is reported in the newspapers, magazines, journals and on the internet concerning the company, the competitors, the industry and the market in general:-

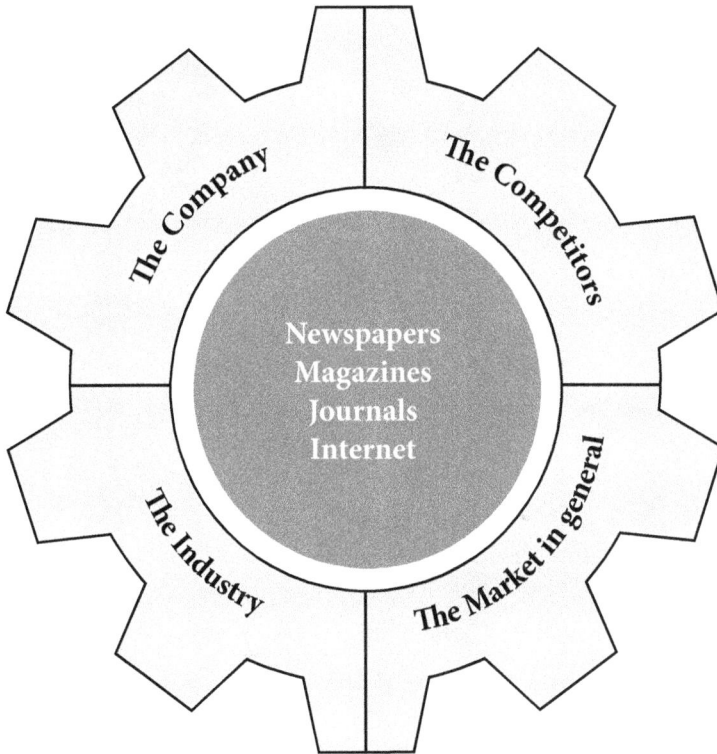

"In the age of technology there is constant access to vast amounts of information.
The basket overflows; people get overwhelmed; the eye of the storm is not so much what goes on in the world, it is the confusion of how to think, feel, digest, and react to what goes on."
– Criss Jami, Venus in Arms

Chapter 8

Thorough Preparation

There is a tremendous amount of preparation required for running a productive and informative meeting. Unfortunately most board members have limited time in which to prepare for a board meeting. Whilst each board member has to prepare individually, the chairman of the board, company secretary and chief executive, should drive the process of a well organised meeting.

The chairman should ensure the high quality of meeting packs and timeous submission. The board must develop meeting protocols which include meeting preparation and attendance, as well as the issue of late board submissions from those who obviously did not allow for thorough preparation.

The chairman must also ensure that each board member thoroughly prepares by emphasising this aspect occasionally. For a new member, the board induction process must provide guidance on thorough preparation and devoting enough time for the board meetings. For existing members, it is important not to assume things but to constantly critically review all information provided. The chairman has to be thoroughly prepared to be exemplary. Thorough preparation facilitates effective participation in the meeting.

> *"By failing to prepare, you are preparing to fail."*
> *– Benjamin Franklin*

The number one irritant in boards either from other board members, from management, through to everyone around the table no matter how junior, is the …

"lack of preparation of board members, who end up asking issues that are in the pack, wanting an explanation of things already explained, wanting to be taken through the pack, thereby using management to prepare, and not applying their minds to issues on the agenda."

All that is expected as a first step is to PREPARE.

Bear in mind that there is preparation, and there is thorough preparation. Is there a difference between the two, and if so, what exactly is the difference?

My understanding is that preparation is about reading what is presented in front of you and occasionally merely browsing through it. After you have prepared for the meeting in this manner, you will at least have an awareness of the issues to be discussed at the meeting, but only that.

Effective board members, though, do not just prepare for meetings, they thoroughly prepare. Why? Because they understand that the war for effectiveness lies beyond just knowing what has been presented to you.

> *"The will to win is nothing without the will to prepare."*
> *– Juma Ikangaa*

What does thorough preparation mean? I understand it to mean going the extra mile to fulfil your responsibility, going beyond the reading the pack supplied by management, even adding at least seven other steps thereafter as explained below:-

Steps towards a Thorough Preparation Process

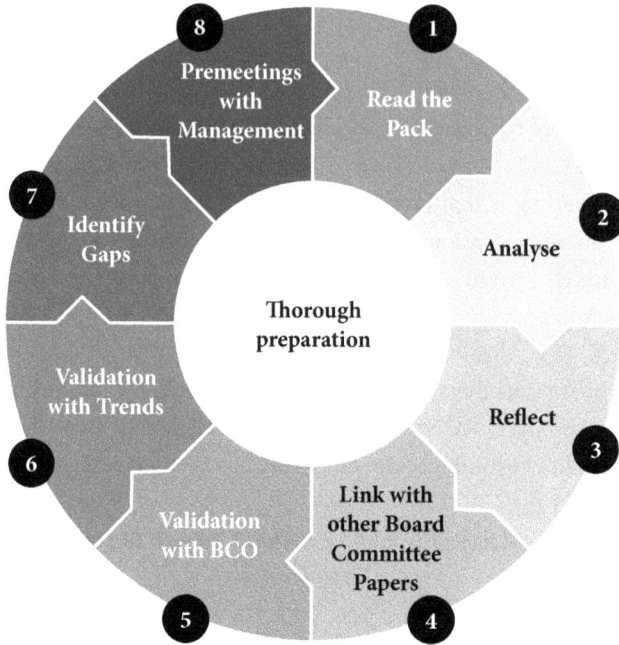

Step 1 – Read the pack

Effective board members read the pack.

Step 2 – Analysis of information provided

Effective board members don't just read the pack, they analyse it.

Step 3 – Reflection on information provided

Effective board members don't just analyse the pack, they reflect upon it.

Step 4 – Link with other board committee papers

Effective board members don't just reflect upon the pack, they link the information with other board committee packs and board papers.

Step 5 – Validation with basic circle of knowledge

Effective board members don't just link the information with other board committee packs and board papers, they validate it with their updated basic circle of knowledge discussed above.

Step 6 - Validation with outward and inward trends

Effective board members don't just validate the pack with their basic circle of knowledge, they also validate with the trends they have observed in the industry and the business.

Step 7 – Identifying missing information

Effective board members don't just validate the pack with trends they have observed in the industry and the business, they also identify the missing issues that should have been included in the pack.

Step 8 – Pre-meeting with management

Effective board members do not just identify missing issues in the pack, they make time for pre-meetings with management to increase their knowledge about the issues at hand. For this reason it is important to develop a board process of raising issues with management prior to the board meeting so that clarity can be sought and obtained even before the main meeting.

"No one ever attains very eminent success by simply doing what is required of him; it is the amount and excellence of what is over and above the required, that determines the greatness of ultimate distinction."
– Anonymous

Chapter 9

Listening & Interrogation

KNOWLEDGE			PARTICIPATION
	Fiduciary Role	Listening & Interrogation	
	The Business	Validation & Contextualisation	
	The Industry	Alertness to Red Flags	
	Up-To-Date Trends	Follow Through	
	Thorough Preparation	Guidance & Resourcefulness	

"I have in mind a person with the intelligence, experience and understanding to know the right questions to ask management or the auditors and the forcefulness and tenacity to ask a direct question and insist on a straight answer. Ideally, all Audit Committee members should have these qualities."
– Commissioner Paul S. Atkins (SEC)

Although this was raised by Commissioner Atkins in the context of audit committee responsibilities this is fully applicable to every director in a company.

As a director is expected to first listen, his or her knowledge processing ability (described in the first part of this quote) is one of the critical success factors for effective participation in board meetings. After that, the director needs the capability to ask and interrogate issues (second part of the quote).

The listening and interrogation phase reflects the beginning of the board discussions.Every director needs to be equipped to best participate in this game.

In each board meeting, every member of management wants to be listened to so that he or she can feel understood (listening skills). Thereafter, if there are issues to be clarified or any blind spots that an executive could have had, he or she needs to hear about it (interrogation skill).

Listening

It is critical that board members listen attentively in meetings.

"There's a lot of difference between listening and hearing."
– G.K. Chesterton

This is true, there is indeed is a big difference between hearing and listening.

Hearing is merely hearing the sounds of the people speaking in the meeting without processing the information internally with an intention of responding. While most people confuse hearing with listening, hearing is only being aware of the sounds around you.

Effective board members do not just hear that people are speaking, they listen to what people are saying.

But what is listening?

Listening in this context means 'hearing the meaning' of what people are saying,
being attentive and inquisitive about what they say, and following up with the speaker to ensure understanding has occurred.

> *"Most people do not listen with the intent to understand; they listen with the intent to reply."*
> *– Stephen R. Covey*

As a director, please make sure you do not fall into the trap of thinking about what next to say when someone is still speaking.

Listen attentively, listen inquisitively, listen to understand.

According to Forbes.com, genuine listening has become a rare gift—the gift of time.

Effective board discussions depend largely on how much genuine listening takes place by management and non-executive directors alike. A director can therefore never excel in his or her responsibility without genuine listening skills.

There are many methods for improving effective listening skills. You may have learnt these some years ago, but in essence, as a director, you need to polish up on your listening skills before you can effectively participate in any board meeting.

Forbes.com continues to provide 10 tips to develop effective listening skills. For your convenience, I quote these tips below:-

Tip 1:   Face the speaker and maintain eye contact.

Tip 2:   Be attentive, but relaxed.

Tip 3:   Keep an open mind.

Tip 4:   Listen to the words and try to picture what the speaker is saying.

Tip 5:   Don't interrupt and don't impose your "solutions."

Tip 6:   Wait for the speaker to pause to ask clarifying questions

Tip 7:   Ask questions only to ensure understanding.

Tip 8:   Try to feel what the speaker is feeling.

Tip 9:   Provide the speaker regular feedback.

Tip 10:   Pay attention to what isn't said, to nonverbal cues.

Interrogation

Interrogation goes beyond just asking a question.

'Asking' is asking for an answer and being grateful for it, whereas interrogation means asking a question, evaluating the answer and following up should there be any gaps or if an answer triggers yet another question.

Effective board members do not ask questions, they interrogate issues. (Kindly take note that you are expected to interrogate 'issues' not 'people', as the end result might be very different.)

Perhaps this can be explained via a simplified (fictitious to illustrate a point) example:-

Asking scenario:-

Question from a director:

I note that we are falling behind budget on our international operations for the second quarter in a row and the local business does not seem to be meeting the set targets for this quarter as well. What is the reason for that?

Answer from the CEO:

Your observation is correct as we seem to be failing to gain traction in international operations for various reasons including the change of leadership on the ground and the inability to increase our market share due to aggressive pricing approach which our competitors apply. From the local business we had operational challenges that slowed us down at a time when we had increased focus to increase performance in our international operations.

Board member:

This does not sound good, what progress has been made to resolve these issues?

Answer from the CEO:

We have made a lot of progress in that we have settled the new team abroad and also increased more attention locally to address the operational challenges we experienced over the last quarter.

Board member:

I hope the results for the third quarter will show improvement.

Interrogation Scenario

Question from an effective board member:

I note that we are falling behind budget on our international operations for the second quarter in a row and the local business does not seem to be meeting the set targets for this quarter as well. What is the reason for that?

Answer from the CEO:

Your observation is correct as we seem to be failing to gain traction in international operations for various reasons including the change of leadership on the ground and the inability to increase our market share due to aggressive pricing approach which our competitors apply. From the local business we had operational challenges that slowed us down at a time when we had increased focus to increase performance in our international operations.

Follow up from the director:

Chairman, based on the answers, allow me follow-up questions on these issues:

1. Why did we experience a change of leadership so soon as my understanding is that we appointed that team less than 18 months ago?

2. What has triggered the aggressive competitive pricing internationally?

3. What strategies are we implementing to gain market share despite the pricing war?

4. What operational challenges have we experienced locally?

5. Why would increased focus on international business prejudice our local success? Is it because we don't have sufficient management bandwidth to adequately manage our group operations?

Answers from the CEO:

Our thinking in terms of what they (divisional MD and the sales director) had to deliver as their KPI's has not been aligned and we are seriously focused on measuring their success based on outcomes than their respective inputs. With them at the helm we continuously lost market share and we therefore had to change the leadership team and could not wait for their five year term to end.

The barriers to entry in this industry are very low unlike locally, and therefore there were two new entrants in the market during the first half of the year. Both of them attracted attention through price cuts and a heavy marketing budget.

We are now focusing on after sales service to increase customer retention and we have introduced a loyalty scheme to improved retention.

This seems to be paying dividends as our sales during the last week are above budget.

Locally we had challenges with our IT system which was relatively unstable and had unplanned revenue leakages at a time when our CIO was focused on international operations.

With the applied interrogation approach as above, this director interrogated the issues and was alert to possible issues which the company needs to pay attention to namely:-

1. Company contracting with key employees without specific KPI's;

2. Company exposed to dollar-based damages for pre-mature cancellation of employment contracts with key employees;

3. Company lacks agility to deal with competitive trends;

4. Company did not have a loyalty programme in a mature industry that survives on customer loyalty;

5. Company heavily reliant on IT for revenue without concrete business continuity should the local system not be available; and

6. Company has inadequate management bandwidth to deal with both local and international plans.

Based on the above gaps identified, different debates and resolutions need to take place and all identified risks mitigated.

The interrogation approach on issues tabled at board meetings is an important capability that every director should possess.

Chapter 10

Validation & Contextualisation

KNOWLEDGE	PARTICIPATION
Fiduciary Role	Listening & Interrogation
The Business	Validation & Contextualisation
The Industry	Alertness to Red Flags
Up-To-Date Trends	Follow Through
Thorough Preparation	Guidance & Resourcefulness

As a director, you will be reading board packs that contain relevant information for making specific decisions. In addition, you will be asking questions and receiving explanations or clarity on issues raised.

The validation and contextualisation phase expects you to pay attention to all written submissions and explanations received in order to start a validation process within your basic circle of knowledge and your general experience as a director. Included in your basic circle of knowledge will be your individual experiences either in your core areas of knowledge or your areas of literacy.

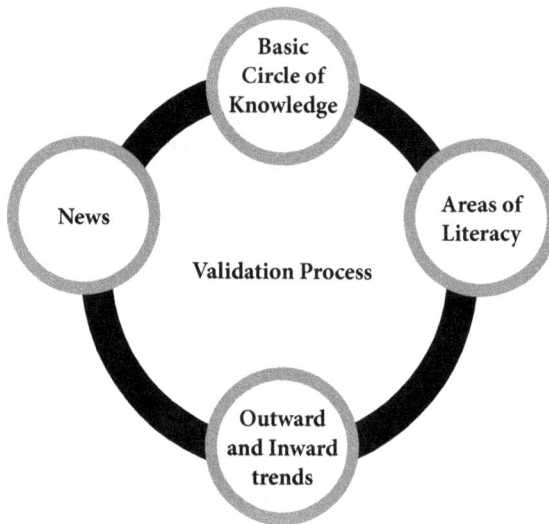

The above diagram illustrates how you validate information at hand with your basic circle of knowledge, your areas of literacy, what you have seen in the news and with your knowledge of outward and inward trends.

A simple and fictitious example can be used to illustrate this.

As a director you note that the tabled budget is based on an exchange rate of $14 and revenue is projected to increase by 15%. During the validation process, you remember that the rand has strengthened back to $11 exchange rate level over the past 24 months. Secondly, in your understanding of the trends most companies in this sector have struggled to achieve more than a single digit growth.

You also understand as a director, that the latest economic data released reflects increased interest rates and increased unemployment, both of which will be detrimental to the demand for the company's products.
This then fails the validation process and therefore as a director you would need more convincing information before participating in any approval process.

Another example to further illustrate the validation process:-

In a board meeting, a director notes that the company does not have a disaster recovery plan. In response, management indicates that this is not a priority given that their systems have never failed them in the past 20 years, and it would be too costly to implement such a plan. They have therefore decided to take a calculated risk.

During the validation process, your core area of knowledge as a director indicates that a disaster recovery plan is a key control; therefore, absorbing this as an accepted risk is still extremely risky for the company.

Secondly, based on previous experiences, you remember that other companies have dealt with this problem successfully and you are also aware, based on your areas of literacy, of new cost-effective strategies in the market for dealing with the current management concern.

Based on the validation process, therefore, as a director you still have to engage management as you cannot accept the explanation received: it fails your validation process.

Another example:-

Management proposed a reduction in the dividend cover to 3 times, as against the 5 times cover of the previous year.

During the validation process, as director you recognise that the company's pressure to reinvest has reduced and the capex expansion programme has normalised. Based on your core area of knowledge, the company's dividend cover can be lower under those circumstances.

Furthermore, as a director you have observed that all other companies in a similar sector have dividend covers that range between 2.5 and 3.5 times and the proposed 3 times cover falls within that range. Based on this reflection, the validation process is passed and you can readily support the proposal tabled by management.

Contextualisation

There is nothing that irritates executives more than directors who continuously offer input that clearly reflects a lack of understanding of the company and the complexity of its processes.

Without fail, almost all members of management become unhappy when directors theorise, that is, provide them with suggestions or demand implementation of things that are not practical within the applicable business environment.

At the same time, as a director you cannot keep quiet in a meeting merely because you are timid and not willing to upset management. Your responsibility as a director is to ensure that whatever input you have is appropriately contextualised to the company at hand, to minimise moments of irrelevance.

This is about ensuring that you apply everything within the context of the company with which you are dealing. The contextualisation process, therefore, encourages board members to understand the business well so that any suggestions, questions or input can be tailor-made to suit the business environment.

During the contextualisation process, a director should check, based on the understanding of the business, if what he or she suggests will be practical for this environment. Moreover, when in doubt, a director must always investigate about the business, and should openly ask for the reasons why the input, which has a successful track record elsewhere, would not be applicable in this particular company.

Example of issues to be considered during the contextualisation phase would include the following:-

- the nature of the business versus the one being compared;
- the sensitivity of the company to the key economic indicators compared to other companies;
- the existing control environment of the company compared to the one from which you wish to draw lessons; and
- the maturity of the labour market and scarcity of critical skills required in evaluating relevance of retention strategies proposed.

Contextualisation using outward trends

Contextualisation would also involve adjusting the outward trends to the business itself. If for example, based on outward trends, a director notes that the reporting trends of most listed companies involve extensive environmental reporting, before a request is made for the company to enhance its level of environmental reporting to new standards, the director has to contextualise that trend to the company by considering whether or not those companies are within the same sector as the company. And if so, if the extent of environmental compliance requires the same level of environmental rehabilitation, reserves and environmental accountability, and so on.

A director can also note that the dividend covers of most companies in a similar sector are much lower than your company's dividend cover. You would limit your effectiveness if, as a director, you would now expect that your company must have a similar dividend cover although your capex expansion programme is different. If your business is on an aggressive expansion programme, it cannot be expected to lower its dividend cover to align with competitors because your growth path as a company might be very different.

Contextualisation based on inward trends

Contextualisation based on inward trends is also necessary because the trends within the business itself are a fair indication of a 'reality check' for everyone. The following three examples illustrate the point. (Kindly note that these examples are fictitious and specific for illustrating the point.)

Example 1:

If the company's budget tabled shows revenue growth of 12% for the next five years, whilst the previous five year's results showed a decline of 2% year on year, and the economic growth is still on the decline, it would not be reasonable for you to be comfortable with the new growth projections that are tabled for your approval. This 12% growth would not pass the contextualisation test when based on inward trends.

Therefore, as a director, you would need to know what the company would be counting on to meet its targets which was not there in the previous five years, and, based contextualisation, you would need to be fully convinced about the company's new capacity to achieve such growth prior to approving this process.

Example 2:

A company tables a business plan for the expansion of its operations in which it is leaning on an 8% margin to be derived from the new operations. When you reflect on the previous margins achieved by the company from the same product range, you realise that the highest margin achieved has been around 4.5% over the last five years. As a director, you would therefore be justified in wanting to understand how the company intends to achieve almost double the margin it wishes to lean on before you can participate in the approval of the business plan presented to the board.

Example 3:

The company is securing replacement funding from a bank and when you notice the covenants they include the following:-

- minimum bank balance of R50 million
- acid test ratio of 1.5:1;
- minimum debt equity ratio of 60:40;
- interest cover ratio of 5:1; and
- no dividend payments until loan is reduced by 50%.

In applying your mind to this as director you recall these company's inward trends:-

- the bank balance has never been greater than R40 million
- the company acid test ratio has never been better than the standard 1:1
- the company debt equity ratio has always varied between 60:40 and 70:30; and
- the company has had a consistent dividend cover of three and your investors are very sensitive to an abrupt change in dividend policy.

These new debt covenants would not pass the contextualisation phase as the company's inward trends indicate the company's difficulty in meeting the debt covenants and therefore attract a going concern threat which will not be in the best interest of the company. As a director, you would therefore be keen to understand more before you participate in the approval process for this replacement funding.

Chapter 11

Alertness to Red Flags

KNOWLEDGE

- Fiduciary Role
- The Business
- The Industry
- Up-To-Date Trends
- Thorough Preparation

PARTICIPATION

- Listening & Interrogation
- Validation & Contextualisation
- Alertness to Red Flags
- Follow Through
- Guidance & Resourcefulness

According to freedictionary.com a red flag is defined as:-

"1. A warning signal.
2. Something that demands attention or provokes an irritated reaction"

In business, a red flag can be defined as "a warning sign: a sign that there is a problem that should be noticed or dealt with". It is important to note that a red flag is something to be alert to, as it is never served up on a silver platter. Red flags might emerge from the board pack submitted, or perhaps emerge during the discussions underway during a meeting. A director must therefore, in the process of preparation and participation in meetings, be alert, keeping eyes and ears open for red flags. And once noted, a director must then influence the discussion in board meetings to pro-actively address these red flags.

There is no one place where a director may encounter red flags, as they can be embedded within the structure of the company; they can be transactional (i.e based on the type of transactions entered into and timing thereof); they may be financial linked to company performance; they may be in the type of suppliers used; or they may even be embedded in the management style of the company.

Overall the ability to identify red flags results from the knowledge phase and the participation phase of B6em. Therefore, knowledge of the business and the industry, understanding the trends, thorough preparation, listening and interrogation and validation and contextualisation of the information presented to you will enable you as a director to develop a keen eye for red flags.

It is therefore impossible to provide a comprehensive list of the red flags a director might come across as these differ from business to business.

Here a list of some examples of red flags is provided for guidance:-

- complex business arrangements, which you fail to understand as a director;
- overly complex organisational structure involving numerous or unusual legal entities;
- widely dispersed business locations with decentralised management and poor internal reporting systems;
- excessive number of bank accounts or subsidiaries or branches in jurisdictions for which there appears to be no business justification.
- a company's downgrading by rating agencies;
- large last minute transactions resulting in significant revenues in half yearly or annual reports. This could be due to the desire to present results for some other intention (e.g. bonuses);
- management's inability to close deals;
- continuous labour disagreements;
- changes in auditors over accounting disagreements;
- overly optimistic news releases without underlying factual developments to back the level of optimism portrayed;
- financial results that are too good to be true or significantly better than competitors without substantive differences in operations;
- inconsistencies between facts and underlying financial statements;
- only a marginal ability to meet debt repayment requirements;
- breach of debt covenants or minimal headroom over covenant levels;
- a consistently close match between actual results and budgeted results;
- evasiveness from management when dealing with questions from directors;
- over domineering personality in management;
- inability to generate cash flows from operations while reporting strong earnings and earnings growth. The board might not be given a complete picture;
- a poor or deteriorating financial position when management have personally guaranteed significant debts of the entity;
- frequent instances of differences in views between management and external auditors;
- use of reserves to smooth out earnings;

- consistent pattern of meeting budgets through close to year-end sales entries;
- significant pressure to obtain additional capital in order to stay competitive;
- inconsistency of management explanations across the company;
- aggressive management behaviour in board meetings;
- failure to enforce company's code of conduct or values;
- regular visits from the regulators;

In addition to the normal business red flags, directors must be attentive for going concern red flags, some of which include the following:-

- negative cash flow from operations;
- loss of key customers or suppliers;
- recurring operating losses;
- cash flow problems such as difficulty in paying overheads;
- serious deterioration in working capital or liquidity ratios;
- difficulty in obtaining new credit;
- breach of loan covenants;
- unfavourable changes to credit terms by suppliers;
- threat of imminent bankruptcy or foreclosure;
- marginal ability to meet debt repayment requirements;
- attempts to raise capital by sale of operating assets;
- work stoppages due to labour disputes;
- loss of access to legal rights or licence to operate conditions.

Chapter 12

Follow Through

To enhance your effectiveness as a director, you must be sure to follow-up and follow-through on issues raised, otherwise your input and effectiveness as a director can depreciate. There are five steps for an effective follow through process in the context of a board meeting including at least the following:-

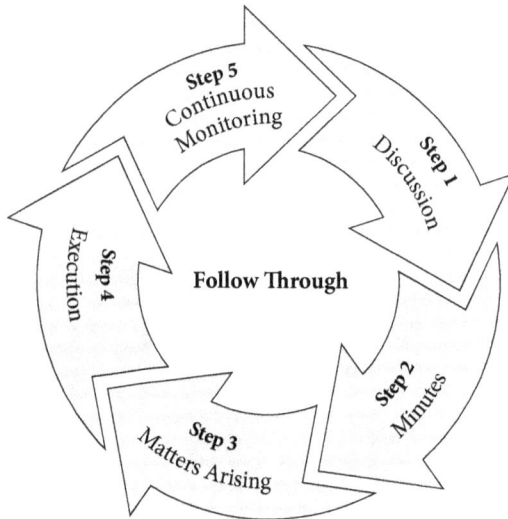

Step 1: Discussion in meetings

There will be times when you will ask questions and receive answers that do not address the questions raised. As a director you have the responsibility of following-up and following-through until answers are clear and satisfactory.

I must warn you that this needs a lot of courage. Practice this concept and you will find out why.

Step 2: Minutes of the meeting

Minutes of the meeting are intended to reflect the correct recording of the proceedings of the previous board or committee meeting. In addition to the general recording of the proceedings, all decisions that are taken that require an action plan must be minuted because if they are not, no one will remember the action plan agreed upon, and no monitoring will take place. As a result, that input or decision or resolution will disintegrate.

Even so, there are times when valid and valuable issues get raised but do not get minuted, and with benefit of the doubt, unintentionally.

As a director you have to be alert to ensure that critical issues discussed, decisions taken and agreed action plans are properly minuted. This is achieved by careful listening and making mental notes or written notes of issues you deem important.

When you review the minutes of the previous meeting, this is when you need to refer to your mental or written notes made during the last board meeting. It might assist you as a director if minutes are circulated shortly after the board meeting whilst issues are still fresh in your mind. This does not happen automatically;- pro-actively requesting this from the chairman of the board is a valuable exercise.

If as a director you dissented on a matter in the previous meeting, you need to follow the matter through by ensuring that the dissent is correctly recorded prior to the approval of the minutes.

Step 3: Matters arising schedule

The matters arising schedule is ideally meant to ensure that all the decisions taken that require action have been acted upon. A schedule generates a platform for directors to monitor the actions taken.

However, three things frequetly go awry with the matters arising schedule:

1. Issues can be recorded as having been resolved, whilst in essence they have not been resolved;

2. Issues can be recorded with inappropriate action plans and the results of the inappropriate action plans considered as satisfactory and therefore resolved; and

3) Issues can be minuted but omitted from the matters arising schedule.

It is director's responsibility to make certain that all issues that require follow up or implementation do appear in the matters arising schedule, and thus the schedule is accurate and complete.

Moreover, a director must pay attention to the detemined action plans to ensure that they are appropriate and precise for resolving the issues at hand. If the action plans are inappropriate or not aligned to the minutes, the matter needs to be raised and flagged as still requiring management attention.

In cases where the issues are labelled as resolved in the matters arising schedule, it is the director's responsibility to analyse the write up and be satisfied that indeed the matter is closed.

Step 4: Execution

Sometimes management provide reports in response to board requests. In some cases, however, these reports might not specifically address the purpose for which they were required.

Directors need to review these reports and provide management with the necessary positive feedback when the objectives are achieved, and advice for improvement in cases when necessary.

Step 5: Continuous follow through

Continuous follow through is constantly required from directors.

If as a director, you continously apply the above diagram, there will be effectiveness from discussions to actions to results.

With consistent follow through, the desirable will happen and every stakeholder will see the results – that is effectiveness!

Chapter 13

○ Guidance & Resourcefulness

KNOWLEDGE		PARTICIPATION
Fiduciary Role	Listening & Interrogation	
The Business	Validation & Contextualisation	
The Industry	Alertness to Red Flags	
Up-To-Date Trends	Follow Through	
Thorough Preparation	Guidance & Resourcefulness	

GUIDANCE

*"Provide people enough guidance to make decisions you
want them to make.
Don't tell them what to do, but encourage them to do what is best."*
– Jimmy Johnson

This quote from Jimmy Johnson is quite appropriate in the context of boards. Directors have to provide enough counsel and guidance to achieve the end result they believe is best for the company.

This is an important phase in the board & Committee Effectiveness Model as some directors might erroneously believe that their role is about policing management and 'catching them out' when they are doing the wrong things.

This is a wrong belief, however, which needs to be discarded.

Management (executive directors) also have the best interest of the company in mind as they share the same risks as non-executive directors. So a bit of guidance here and there might assist management in adhering to best practice in terms of governance, strategy, operations and business funding model. This is because as a non-executive director, you have the advantage of learning the best from other companies to which you are exposed, and instead of criticising management unnecessarily, you can simply provide the guidance to contribute to the achievement of the company's objectives. This is an advantage that executive directors do not have as their main deliverable is to focus on the day to day running of the business.

It is important, therefore, that directors should adopt a powerful partnership approach with management and ensure that the best synergies will be derived from this relationship.

As a director, do not only ask for explanations, but provide guidance where there is clearly a need. As an example;-

- Management can be guided based on your basic circle of knowledge.
- Management can be guided based on best practice you have been exposed to.
- Management can be guided to be proactive based on trends witnessed elsewhere.

RESOURCEFULNESS

According to Oxford Dictionaries.com, being resourceful means,

"having the ability to find quick and clever ways to overcome difficulties"

There are a variety of difficult situations that the board will need to deal with. Each director has an opportunity to contribute towards the resolution of any and all matters at hand.

Executives do enjoy tapping into the wisdom of the directors as that helps them deal with the blind spots they were unaware of, and they arrive at much more effective solutions than they could have got on their own.

When directors openly share their wisdom and experience for resolving problems the company is facing, then the executives experience a distinct 'value-add' and will eagerly anticipate upcoming board meetings. Once executives look forward to a board meeting, then the magic begins: a powerful partnership that unleashes great potential and success on behalf of the company and its stakeholders!

"Life is too short to hang out with people who are not resourceful".
– Jeff Bezos

Conclusion

"If we encounter a man of rare intellect, we should ask him what books he reads."
– Ralph Waldo Emerson

Most people never allocate time to read, and even if they do, they rarely finish what they have started to read. That is why Ralph Emerson believes that men of rare intellect are definitely readers.

Having read this book until the end, now with the full knowledge of BCem, you have an opportunity of being classified as a man or woman of rare intellect, a man or woman capable of excelling as an effective director from the very first board meeting or board committee meeting you attend.

Congratulations!

After completing this book, I read it over and over again, and the more I read it, the more I am convinced that if I knew anything about this Board & Committee Effectiveness Model (BCem) in the early 90s, I would have been an effective director from my very first participation as a director in a board meeting.

I therefore have no doubt, in fact I am very certain that any inexperienced director, or any director in fact who wishes to participate in the effective director league will be guaranteed results from applying the principles of this book.

As a director with a full understanding of your flight plan, I can only imagine how confident you are to take off using your aircraft that is filled to capacity with plenty of jet fuel for your journey as a director. You know your current capabilities and your level of knowledge, and you know your destination. You know your altitude level, you know the aerospace, both restricted and unrestricted, you know the weather and you are ready to adjust your plan depending on the direction of the wind. Last but not least, you also know the alternative airports you will land in should you have emergencies.

The application of the principles herein remains a critical path in your journey to being an effective director. The following quote by William Phelps emphasises the need to read with results.

"I divide all readers into two classes; those who read to remember and those who read to forget."
– William Lyon Phelps

If you forget any element of the knowledge phase or participation phase, please read this book over and over again.

"There's nothing wrong with reading a book you love over and over."
– Gail Carson Levine

I am now leaving you this Model to view time and time again. Be certain you don't forget it!

The Board & Committee Effectiveness Model (BCem)

KNOWLEDGE		PARTICIPATION
Fiduciary Role		Listening & Interrogation
The Business		Validation & Contextualisation
The Industry		Alertness to Red Flags
Up-To-Date Trends		Follow Through
Thorough Preparation		Guidance & Resourcefulness

www.ingramcontent.com/pod-product-compliance
Lightning Source LLC
Chambersburg PA
CBHW071459200326
41519CB00019B/5803